Wake up to your inner courage and become steeped in divine contentment

A Book of Contemplations

Wake up to your inner courage and become steeped in divine contentment

A SIDDHA YOGA PUBLICATION
PUBLISHED BY SYDA FOUNDATION

Published by SYDA Foundation
371 Brickman Rd., P.O. Box 600,
South Fallsburg, New York 12779, USA

Acknowledgments
Our unalloyed appreciation and delight go to Cheryl Crawford for the design, to Stéphane Dehais for typesetting, to Sushila Traverse and Valerie Ann Sensabaugh for overseeing production, and to the researchers — Valerie Boyd, Gali Kronenberg, Anandi Seigrist, Gloria Staackmann, and Marianne Vie — for their contributions to the text.

—*Swami Anantananda and Ellen Porter*

Copyright © 1997 SYDA Foundation.® All rights reserved

No part of this book may be reproduced or transmitted in any form or by any means electronic or mechanical, including photocopy, recording, or any information storage and retrieval system, without permission in writing from SYDA Foundation, Permissions Department, 371 Brickman Rd., P.O. Box 600, South Fallsburg NY 12779-0600, USA.

(Swami) MUKTANANDA, (Swami) CHIDVILASANANDA, GURUMAYI, SIDDHA YOGA, and SIDDHA MEDITATION are registered trademarks of SYDA Foundation.®

Printed in the United States of America

First published 1997

97 98 99 00 01 02   5 4 3 2 1

Library of Congress Catalog Card Number: 97-66735

ISBN 0-911307-55-9

Permissions appear on pages 66-67.

Printed on Recycled Paper

Contents

The Siddha Yoga Tradition ~ vii
Foreword ~ ix
Introduction ~ xv

Part 1
Wake up to your inner courage

Part 2
Become steeped in divine contentment

Glossary ~ 59
Authors and Scriptures ~ 61

The Siddha Yoga Tradition

Siddha Yoga is a path of spiritual unfoldment that is inspired by the grace and guidance of an enlightened Master, known as a Siddha Guru.

A Siddha Guru is one who has the power and knowledge to give others the inner experience of God. Through the transmission of grace, known as *shaktipāt* initiation, the Siddha Master awakens a seeker's inner spiritual energy. Having walked the spiritual path to its final goal, Siddha Gurus dedicate their lives to helping others complete the same journey.

Swami Chidvilasananda, widely known as Gurumayi, is a Siddha Guru. Since early childhood, she has been a disciple of the Siddha Master Swami Muktananda Paramahamsa (1908~1982). It was he who invested Swami Chidvilasananda with the knowledge, power, and authority of the ancient tradition of Siddhas.

During the course of his lifetime, Swami Muktananda became adept at many of the classical paths of yoga, yet he said his spiritual journey did not truly begin until Bhagawan Nityananda, one of the great saints of modern India, awakened him to the experience of the supreme Power within himself.

Bhagawan Nityananda chose Swami Muktananda as his successor and directed him to bring *shaktipāt* initiation and the timeless practices of yoga to seekers everywhere. The path Swami Muktananda taught, which introduced the wisdom and disciplines of ancient sages to the modern world, came to be known as Siddha Yoga. Gurumayi continues her Guru's tradition, offering the teachings of the Siddhas and *shaktipāt* initiation to seekers around the world.

Through Siddha Yoga and its principal practices of meditation, chanting, mantra repetition, contemplation, and selfless service, thousands of people from many different traditions and cultures have discovered within themselves the source of lasting happiness and peace: the experience that we are not separate from God.

Foreword

From the most ancient of times, teachers in the various religious traditions of the world have instructed spiritual seekers to practice a special kind of contemplation in which aspirants read or listen attentively to concise passages of scripture or to powerful words of sages. Seekers then quietly and with deep reverence reflect on the inner significance of the teachings and search within themselves for ways to apply those lessons in their own lives.

In Christian monasticism, for example, monks and nuns who yearn for a taste of God's presence practice what is known as *lectio divina*, holy reading, in which they prayerfully meditate on short passages from scripture as a way to gain inspiration and deeper wisdom. Tradition regards the imbibing of sacred truths in this way as nourishment of the soul and in fact quite vividly describes the process as *ruminatio*, literally a slow and repeated chewing of the sacred words that leads to the release of their full flavor.

In India, such rumination on a sacred text or lesson from one's spiritual teacher may be said to lead to the tasting of *rasa*, the ambrosial essence of the sublime. According to Abhinavagupta, the great Kashmiri Siddha of the eleventh century, *rasāsvāda* is similar to *brahmāsvāda*: the taste of such an essence is comparable to the taste of the Divine itself.

But virtually all religious traditions in India hold that such a nectarean flavor cannot be tasted without diligent and attentive spiritual discipline. Such discipline necessarily includes a number of different yet related practices, one of the most honored of which has always been that of *svādhyāya*, a term we may translate as "self-reflection" or "recitation by oneself." Undertaking *svādhyāya*, a spiritual seeker quietly chants mantras, recites *sūtras*, sings sacred *gītās*, studies texts, or repeats words spoken by the Guru. While doing so, he or she inwardly contemplates their deeper meaning.

The *Bhagavad Gītā* reports Krishna's teaching to Arjuna that *svādhyāya* is one of the divine virtues. In the second century B.C., the great sage Patanjali saw *svādhyāya* to be so important that he listed it among five primary yogic disciplines without which there can be no true spiritual growth (the other four are moral and physical purity, the cultivation of inner contentment or equanimity, fervent dedication to one's practice, and devotion to God). Patanjali taught that *svādhyāya* joins with fervent practice and devotion to God to form what he called the "yoga of action" and that the study of sacred words is such an effective practice that it leads to communion with the Divine. In roughly the eighth century, the teacher Vedavyasa similarly asserted that "the gods, the visionary seers, and the Siddhas themselves become visible to one who practices *svādhyāya.*"

But the spiritual traditions of India also hold that, having heard or read a powerful teaching, a seeker must endeavor to bring the liberating insights and transformative truths presented by those words into effect in his or her life. Otherwise the words merely entertain, mystify, or even clutter the mind. The Siddhas teach us that true contemplation is part of a process: hearing, contemplating, understanding, imbibing, becoming. As Swami Muktananda has said, "Knowledge that is not put into action is a burden."

The contemplations in this book are tools to help you in your own version of *svādhyāya*. You may wish to focus on one particular passage for a period of time. Memorize it, perhaps, or write it down so that you can carry it with you wherever you go. Record your thoughts inspired by the wisdom reflected in these teachings; you will surely delight in the bright gems you thus have mined from the quiet integrity of your own soul.

This collection is part of a series, each book of which contains a set of contemplations centered on a different aspect of the spiritual life. These contemplations are not merely pleasant or interesting thoughts; they are selections from scriptures as well as lessons from philosophers and teachings from ancient and modern saints. They possess *śabda-vīrya*, the "potency of sacred words," the power of which can transform your life and strengthen your spiritual discipline.

Contemplating them, we somehow inwardly recognize the Truth these words outwardly express. This is because the same Truth lies within each of us. It may be that much of the time that Truth is, for us, still vague and unformed because we have not found the words with which to express it. These contemplations give us those words. Reflecting on them can therefore inspire the awakening and blossoming of our own inner wisdom.

Ruminate slowly on these teachings. Relish their delectable essence. Let them nourish you.

William K. Mahony
Department of Religion
Davidson College
Davidson, North Carolina

Introduction

The theme for this set of contemplations comes from Gurumayi Chidvilasananda's New Year's message for 1997: "Wake up to your inner courage and become steeped in divine contentment."

With this message, Gurumayi has given us a superb teaching we can bring into every moment of our lives. The lesson consists of two parts. The first, "Wake up to your inner courage," draws us deeper into the spiritual life; the second, "and become steeped in divine contentment," shows us the valuable consequence of that way of being. Recognition of our inner strength leads to fulfillment, and fulfillment strengthens our fearlessness. As Gurumayi says, "These two qualities, courage and contentment, go together. One is born from the other."

But in order to experience the full truth of this lesson, we must first awaken to the presence of Divinity within the heart, the home and source of both courage and contentment. The very words Gurumayi uses in her message remind us of this fact. The English word *courage* derives from the French *coeur*, which means "heart." And when we look at the origin of the word *contentment*, we see that it means to be the content of something, to be contained by something. Wise teachers throughout history have taught that we are contained by God's unwavering love for us, and that this eternal Presence dwells within the heart. Turning inward to God, we thereby return to our own courage and become infused with contentment.

Life will always have its challenges, for the world is complicated and our lives are filled with uncertainty and with the poignancy of love in our relationships with others and with God. Things will not always be the way the wishes of our ego would want them to be. At these times, as at all times, we must draw on our courage, our innate strength, that Gurumayi reminds us comes from a place beyond desires. In order to be content, we must have courage.

Gurumayi urges us to become *steeped* in contentment. Again, what a wonderful choice of a word! To be steeped in something is to be saturated and cleansed and infused by it. Allowing our ego to dissolve, we become filled with God's abiding love and power. Then we are able to meet each splendid moment of our lives with undaunted courage and true contentment.

The passages in this book come from a number of teachers and religious traditions throughout history. Like Gurumayi's New Year's message itself, which is intentionally the source of all her quotations, the other selections reveal the graceful interplay between inner courage and divine contentment. The lessons in the first section direct our contemplation to the importance of courage. Those in the second section remind us of the result such fearlessness brings: we become imbued in our innate contentment, which is the nature of the divine Self.

As you immerse yourself in these teachings, may they cleanse and refresh your soul.

WKM

Part 1

Wake up
TO YOUR INNER COURAGE

Waking up to your own courage is actually a matter of waking up to the light of the Truth within you. An awakening like that demands your firm determination and the touch of grace.

— SWAMI CHIDVILASANANDA

*Be strong and take heart,
all you who hope in the Lord.*

— BOOK OF PSALMS

Realize the true nature of the ātman, the Self, as the sum of all bliss. Shake off the delusion which your own mind has created. Become free and content. Wake up!

— SHANKARACHARYA

Be strong and enter into your own body: for there your foothold is firm. Consider it well, O my heart! Go not elsewhere. Kabir says: Put all imaginations away and stand fast in that which you are.

— KABIR

Courage is a state that quickens, sustains, and activates this innate life of the spirit, and invigorates the soul's ceaseless aspiration for the Divine.

— ST. MAXIMUS THE CONFESSOR

Cast yourself into the arms of God and be very sure that if He wants anything of you, He will fit you for the work and give you strength.

— PHILIP NERI

One who is inspired by the Self, one whose Self pulsates all the time, becomes great and courageous. In Shaivism it is said, "One who receives inspiration from the Self is very brave. Such a person becomes God." Receive strength and inspiration from the Self.

— SWAMI MUKTANANDA

Remember always that you came here for no other reason than to be a saint; thus let nothing reign in your soul that does not lead you to sanctity.

— ST. JOHN OF THE CROSS

Recognize that you have the courage within you to fulfill the purpose of your birth. Summon forth the power of your inner courage and live the quality of life of your dreams.

— SWAMI CHIDVILASANANDA

Until you meet the pure One,
keep fighting courageously.
If you fear adversity
and shrink from the spiritual battle,
you will be confronted with obstacles
wherever you go.

— SWAMI MUKTANANDA

The first stage on the path of seeking is humility. The great ones say: Humility is the messenger from God to man. Sown in the heart, it impels to God. Practiced for some time, it turns into courage. Masters unanimously hold that love cannot be contained without courage.

— MAKHDUM-UL-MULK

Let nothing perturb you,
nothing frighten you.
All things pass;
God does not change.
Patience achieves everything.
Whoever has God lacks nothing.
God alone suffices.

— ST. TERESA OF AVILA

*Fragrant, delicious fruit is hidden
within every occurrence of every kind.
Have the courage to find
the best outcome in every situation.*

— SWAMI CHIDVILASANANDA

Satisfaction is quietness of heart under the course of destiny.

— AL-MUHASIBI

*This is courage in a human being:
to bear unflinchingly what heaven sends.*

— EURIPIDES

*God likes this kind of devotion:
to live as He keeps you.*

— TUKARAM MAHARAJ

*There is no cheerfulness like the resolution
of a brave mind that has fortune under its feet.
It is an invincible greatness of mind not to be
elevated or dejected with good or ill fortune.
A wise man is content with his lot, whatever
it be — without wishing for what he has not.*

— SENECA

*O*ne who is truly brave and courageous in a spiritual sense, a true seeker, will find it impossible to sleep for even a minute longer than is absolutely necessary.
He will not be a victim of sloth or laziness, nor will he be tormented by his senses.

— SWAMI MUKTANANDA

Nature does not lose her great peace because of the advent of extreme heat or cold, wind or rain, storm or earthquake; rather does she make use of them to quicken the life of her creatures.

— KAIBARA EKKEN

Steadfastness is that courage by means of which a person wouldn't close the eye of clear perception even if the heavens were to fall.

— JNANESHWAR MAHARAJ

Sometimes we are unduly excited when things go well, and at other times we are too alarmed when things go badly. . . . We ought to establish our hearts firmly in God's strength, and struggle, as best we can, to place all our hope and confidence in the Lord so that we shall be like Him, as far as it is possible, even in His unchanging rest and stability.

— JORDAN OF SAXONY

Courage itself consists in persisting in every good work and in overcoming the passions of the soul and body.

— ST. PETER OF DAMASCUS

Valor is the conquest of one's own self.

— SHRIMAD BHAGAVATAM

Hurt no one.
If you plant fear in others,
you will never become fearless.
If you make others dauntless,
fear will not touch you.
You will attain victory.

— SWAMI MUKTANANDA

*Be strong and of good courage;
be not afraid, neither be thou dismayed:
for the Lord thy God is with thee
whithersoever thou goest.*
— JOSHUA

When you meditate and pray to God wholeheartedly, guidance will arise spontaneously within you.

— SWAMI MUKTANANDA

*And if He closes before you
   all the ways and passes,
He will show you a hidden way
   which nobody knows.*
                                    — RUMI

Waking up to your inner courage makes you self-reliant. Courage is an exquisite spark of the infinite light of the Truth. And when you call on the Truth, the power of God at the core of your being takes you across. Having courage is invoking God's power within yourself.

— SWAMI CHIDVILASANANDA

The treasure of the bliss of Brahman is guarded by a very powerful terrible serpent called ahamkāra, ego, coiling around it with its three fierce hoods. The brave one should cut asunder the three heads with the great and sharp sword of wisdom and, destroying this serpent, enjoy this treasure which makes for bliss.

— SHANKARACHARYA

Physical strength depends mainly on spiritual strength. Food can give only a little strength. But the strength that flows from enthroning God in the heart belongs to the spirit and is really great.

— SWAMI MUKTANANDA

In every heart Thou art hidden; in every heart burns Thy light. The Guru's message bursts open the granite doors to salvation, revealing the fearless One entranced in profound meditation.

— GURU NANAK

Awake, my dear.
Be kind to your sleeping heart.
Take it out into the vast fields of Light
And let it breathe.

— HAFIZ

Part 2

Become steeped in divine contentment

Courage must come from a place beyond desires, a place that is rich in wisdom and wholeness. That place is contentment, the deep sense of being in the great heart of God.

Contentment is understanding what is yours and what is not yours, knowing that everything belongs to God and resting in this wisdom.

— SWAMI CHIDVILASANANDA

What is contentment? To renounce all craving for what is not obtained unsought and to be satisfied with what comes unsought. Without being elated or depressed even by them — this is contentment.

— VASISHTHA

There is no calamity greater than lavish desires. There is no greater source of guilt than desire for gain, no greater disaster than greed. He who is content with contentment is always content.

— LAO TZU

Desire can never know contentment. Just as darkness cannot comprehend the sun, desire can never experience satisfaction or fulfillment. In the kingdom of desires, satisfaction and contentment have never taken birth.

— SWAMI MUKTANANDA

*Through contentment
there is a world within my heart.*

— RUMI

*A life filled with work,
contentment in what you have,
a strong sense of duty,
those are the gates to the temple of peace.*

— SWAMI MUKTANANDA

When the day was over
  we lighted our lamp.
The temple bells announced
  the beginning of evening.
Suddenly I realized that quietude
  is indeed joy,
And I felt that my life
  has abundant leisure.

— WANG WEI

With the rise of contentment, the purity of one's heart blooms. The contented one who possesses nothing owns the world.

— VASISHTHA

The yogi's power of forgiveness is like that of the earth, and he holds contentment in his lap.

— JNANESHWAR MAHARAJ

Be contented with your achievements in affairs of the spirit, as well as with your worldly status.

— RABBI MENACHEM MENDEL THE VITEBSKER

Once you taste contentment and start to live in its beauty, you actually want this river of grace to overflow its banks. And that gives you the courage to move forward and make the most of this gift of life.

Life — which is full of difficulties and expectations, full of glory, challenges, promises, purposes, rewards, and failures. Life — which is liberating, which lets us create our freedom. Life — which is the gateway to enlightenment.

— SWAMI CHIDVILASANANDA

Remain quiet.
Discover the harmony in your own being.
Embrace it.
If you can do this, you will gain everything,
And the world will be healthy again.

— LAO TZU

Those who think of Me, who absorb their lives in Me, enlightening each other, and speaking of Me constantly, they are content and rejoice.

— LORD KRISHNA IN THE BHAGAVAD GĪTĀ

When I love a devotee, I, the Lord, become his ear so that he hears through Me. I become his eye so that he sees through Me, I become his tongue so that he speaks through Me, and I become his hand so that he possesses through Me.

— DHU-AL-NUN

Contentment arises from knowing that
you are with God and God is with you.
This experience must be constantly renewed.
Then your contentment is always fresh
like the dawn and new like the beginning
of each year.

— SWAMI CHIDVILASANANDA

When you drink from the stream, remember the source.

— CHINESE PROVERB

I can love you more than you can love yourself, and I watch over you a thousand times more carefully than you can watch over yourself. The more trustfully you give yourself up to Me, the more I shall be watching over you; you will gain a clearer knowledge of Me and experience My love more and more joyfully.

— CATHERINE OF SIENA

I roar! Oh, and I dance!
My heart's desires are fulfilled
Now that You, Lord,
Infinitely splendid,
Have come to me.

— UTPALADEVA

*My soul rests in You.
All else is emptiness.*

— TUKARAM MAHARAJ

The minute you turn to the source of grace, the minute you turn to the infinite light of God in your heart, you find all the peace and all the protection you need.

— SWAMI CHIDVILASANANDA

Contentment is indeed the highest heaven, supreme joy. There is no higher satisfaction. It is complete in itself.

— MAHĀBHĀRATA

Glossary

ahamkāra: Ego; that which creates the experience of limited individuality.

ātman: Divine Consciousness residing in the individual; the supreme Self; the soul.

Brahman: In Vedantic philosophy, the absolute Reality or all-pervasive supreme Principle of the universe.

Self: *See ātman.*

Shaivism: Also known as Kashmir Shaivism; a branch of the Shaivite philosophical tradition that explains how the formless supreme Principle, Shiva, manifests as the universe.

Authors and Scriptures

Al-Muhasibi (781~837) Born at Basra; founder of the Baghdad school of mysticism. His best known work is the *Ri aya*, a manual of the inner life.

Bhagavad Gītā (lit., song of the Lord) One of the world's great spiritual texts and an essential scripture of India in which Lord Krishna instructs his disciple Arjuna on the nature of the universe, God, and the supreme Self.

Catherine of Siena (1347~1380) Dominican mystic and patron saint of Italy; she played a large part in returning the papacy from Avignon to Rome. In 1970, she was declared a doctor of the church.

Dhu-al-Nun (796~859) Egyptian Sufi poet-saint. In 829 he was imprisoned for heresy, but during his trial, Dhu-al-Nun so moved the caliph with his defense of Sufism that he was released unharmed.

Ekken, Kaibara (1629~1713) Japanese scholar and teacher of royal princes who, on his seventieth birthday, retired to write a number of books on meditation.

Euripides (5th century B.C.) Poet and playwright who lived in Phyla, near Athens, Greece.

Guru Nanak (1469~1538) Founder and first Guru of the Sikh religion; he sought to combine Hindu and Muslim elements in a single creed.

Hafiz (1326~1390) Persian Sufi lyric poet who worked as a court poet and a college professor. His tomb has been a place of pilgrimage for over six hundred years.

Jnaneshwar Maharaj (1275~1296) Great poet-saint of India whose *Jnaneshwari* is a magnificent commentary in Marathi verse on the *Bhagavad Gītā*.

John of the Cross, Saint (1542~1591) Spanish mystic and poet whose best known works include *The Spiritual Canticle* and *The Dark Night of the Soul*.

Jordan of Saxony (d. 1237) Born in Germany and educated in Paris; he became Master of the Order of Preachers in 1222, and under his leadership the order entered a period of expansion.

Joshua (Hebrew: Yehoshua) Celebrated for his faithfulness and courage, he was the successor to Moses and leader of Israel in the conquest and settlement of the Promised Land.

Kabir (1440~1518) Poet and saint who worked as a simple weaver in Benares. His followers included both Hindus and Muslims, and his influence was a powerful force in overcoming religious factionalism.

Krishna, Lord Eighth incarnation of Lord Vishnu,

whose spiritual teachings are contained in the *Bhagavad Gītā*.

Lao Tzu (6th century B.C.) Chinese philosopher and purported author of the classic scripture of Taoism, *Tao Te Ching* ("The Way and Its Power").

Mahābhārata Epic poem recounting the struggle between the Kaurava and Pandava brothers over a disputed kingdom; contains a wealth of Indian secular and religious lore, and is the setting for the crown jewel of Indian scriptures, the *Bhagavad Gītā*.

Makhdum-Ul-Mulk (15th century) Eminent Sufi master of Behar, India; author of *Maktubat-e-sadi*, a collection of one hundred letters covering topics of spiritual training.

Maximus the Confessor, Saint (580~662) Born in Constantinople, he left the service of Emperor Heraclius to live a monastic life in Asia Minor and North Africa. His writings provided the foundation for most Byzantine mysticism.

Neri, Philip (1515~1595) Italian priest and mystic who attracted disciples from all walks of life and renewed the religious life of Rome.

Peter of Damascus, Saint (12th century) Monk of the orthodox Christian tradition whose writings are included in the Philokalia. While writing primarily for monks, Peter claimed that salvation and spiritual knowledge are within the reach of everyone.

Rabbi Menachem Mendel the Vitebsker (18th century) Leading disciple of the Ba'al Shem Tov; he moved to Palestine and continued the Hassidic teachings there.

Rumi, Jalaluddin (1207~1273) The most eminent saint of Persia and Turkey; he was transformed from a sober scholar to an intoxicated lover of God after one meeting with his Master, Shams-i-Tabriz.

Seneca (4 B.C.~65 C.E.) Roman statesman and philosopher, tutor to Nero; he wrote many poetic and prose works.

Shankaracharya (780~820) Venerated sage who spread the philosophy of Advaita Vedanta, absolute non-dualism, throughout India. His best known work is *Viveka Chudamani*, "The Crest Jewel of Discrimination."

Shrīmad Bhāgavatam One of the Puranas, consisting of ancient legends of the various incarnations of the Lord; contains the life of Lord Krishna and stories of the sages and their disciples.

Teresa of Avila, Saint (1515~1582) Spanish Catholic mystic who founded and supervised seventeen convents in a period of twenty years. Her best known works, in which she shares the fruits of her years of contemplation, are *The Interior Castle* and *The Way of Perfection*.

Tukaram Maharaj (1608~1650) Poet-saint who lived as a grocer in Maharashtra, India; he wrote thousands of devotional songs describing his spiritual experiences, the realization of God, and the glory of the divine Name.

Utpaladeva (900~950) Enlightened Kashmir Shaivite philosopher and author of *Shivastotravali*, "Garland of Songs to Shiva."

Vasishtha Legendary sage and Guru of Lord Rama who, in the *Yoga Vasishtha*, answers Lord Rama's questions on life, death, and human suffering by teaching that the world is as you see it and that illusion ceases when the mind is stilled.

Wang Wei (699~761) Devout Chinese Buddhist landscape painter and writer of simple mystic poems.

Copyright Acknowledgments and Permissions

We gratefully acknowledge the following sources:

p. 6: Rabindranath Tagore, trans., *Songs of Kabir* (York Beach, Maine: Samuel Weiser, Inc., 1995).

p. 7: *The Philokalia*, vol 2, (London: Faber & Faber Ltd, 1981).

p. 14: Stephen Clissold, *Wisdom of the Spanish Mystics* (Copyright 1977 by Stephen Clissold). Reprinted by permission of New Directions Publishing Corporation.

p. 21: Kaibara Ekken, *The Way of Contentment*, trans. by Ken Hoshino (London: John Murray, 1913).

pp. 22, 45: Swami Kripananda, *Jnaneshwar's Gita* (Albany, N.Y.: SUNY Press, 1989). Reprinted by permission of SUNY Press.

p. 24: *The Philokalia*, vol 3, (London: Faber & Faber Ltd, 1984).

p. 34: Annemarie Schimmel, *Mystical Dimensions of Islam* Copyright © 1978 by the University of North Carolina Press. Used by permission of the publisher.

p. 34: *I Heard God Laughing, Renderings of Hafiz* by Daniel Ladinsky, published by Sufism Reoriented, Walnut Creek, Calif. Reprinted by permission of author.

p. 41: Camille and Kabir Helminski, trans., *Daylight* (Putney, Vermont: Threshold Books, 1994). Reprinted by permission.

p. 43: Chang Chung-Yuan, *Creativity and Taoism* (New York: Julian Press, 1963).

p. 48: Brian Walker, trans., *Hua Hu Ching* (New York: HarperCollins, 1992). Reprinted by permission of author.

p. 49: Winthrop Sargeant, *Shri Bhagavad Gita* (Albany, N.Y.: SUNY Press, 1993). Reprinted by permission of SUNY Press.

p. 50: Llewellyn Vaughan-Lee, *Traveling the Path of Love* (Inverness, Calif.: The Golden Sufi Center, 1995). Reprinted by permission.

p. 54: Constantina Rhodes Bailly, *Meditations on Shiva: The Shivastotravali of Utpaladeva* (Albany, N.Y.: SUNY Press, © 1995). Reprinted by permission of SUNY Press.

p. 55: Dilip Chitre, *Says Tuka* (New Delhi: Penguin Books Ltd., 1991). Reprinted by permission.

Further Reading

SWAMI MUKTANANDA

Play of Consciousness
Bhagawan Nityananda of Ganeshpuri
From the Finite to the Infinite
Where Are You Going?
I Have Become Alive
The Perfect Relationship
Selected Essays
Reflections of the Self
Secret of the Siddhas
Light on the Path
I Am That
Ashram Dharma
Kundalini
Mystery of the Mind
Does Death Really Exist?
Lalleshwari
Meditate
What Is an Intensive?

SWAMI CHIDVILASANANDA

Enthusiasm

The Yoga of Discipline

My Lord Loves a Pure Heart

Inner Treasures

Kindle My Heart

Ashes at My Guru's Feet

CONTEMPLATION BOOKS

The Magic of the Heart
Reflections on Divine Love

Resonate with Stillness
*Daily contemplations from the words of
Swami Muktananda, Swami Chidvilasananda*

Be Filled with Enthusiasm and Sing God's Glory

Blaze the Trail of Equipoise

Everything Happens for the Best

You may learn more about the teachings and practices of Siddha Yoga meditation by contacting:

SYDA Foundation
371 Brickman Rd.
P.O. Box 600
South Fallsburg, NY 12779-0600, USA

Tel: (914) 434-2000

or

Gurudev Siddha Peeth
P.O. Ganeshpuri
PIN 401 206
District Thana
Maharashtra, India

For further information on books in print by Swami Muktananda and Swami Chidvilasananda, and editions in translation, please contact:

Siddha Yoga Meditation Bookstore
371 Brickman Rd.
P.O. Box 600
South Fallsburg, NY 12779-0600, USA

Tel: (914) 434-2000 ext. 1700